Big Pink Umbrella
Susan Millar DuMars

salmonpoetry

Published in 2008 by
Salmon Poetry,
Cliffs of Moher, County Clare, Ireland
Website: www.salmonpoetry.com
Email: info@salmonpoetry.com

ISBN 978-1-903392-74-4

Cover photograph: Claude Madec
Cover design & typesetting: Siobhán Hutson

For Karma
1986-2006

Acknowledgments

Acknowledgements are due to the editors of the following, in which some of the poems in this collection first appeared: *Arrowsmith; The Burning Bush; Crannóg; Earth's Daughters; Exposure; The Galway Advertiser; The Mag; Markings; Nth Position Website; On San Francisco Magazine; Other Voices Website; Oxygen; Poetry Motel; Rattapallax/Short Fuse Website; ROPES; The SHOp.*

"Honey" appeared in the *Gateway Poetry Anthology*. "Shirt", "Winter Eggs", "Home from Work", "Open Palms", "Fallen 1973", "Cathal Briefly", "Honey" and "Knowing About Your Life" appeared in *Anthology I* (Ainnir).

"Shirt" made the finals of the Rattlebag/Dublin Writers' Festival Poetry Slam 2003 and was broadcast on RTE One Radio. "My Husband the Great Poet" made the finals of the Cuírt Grand Slam 2006. "What Seems To Be The Problem?" came third in the North Beach Nights Grand Slam 2007.

Several of these poems appeared in the chapbook *Everyone Loves Me* (Lapwing Press, 2005).

I'm deeply grateful to Jessie Lendennie and Siobhán Hutson of Salmon Poetry, as well as all the Salmon poets I've recently met, for welcoming me to the family. Warm thanks to Claude Madec for the cover photograph; and to poets Lorna Shaughnessy and Celeste Augé for their peerless editorial support. Thanks as well to Dennis Greig; the women of the Thursday workshop at Galway Arts Centre; and to The Writers' Keep for their feedback on these poems. My love and thanks to my family, especially those unsung members, Cathy and Bobby. And finally, for Kevin, my veggie chilli and devotion forever. Amen.

Contents

PART TWO

Part One

Fallen 1973

Jesus – a snappy dresser
in cranberry velvet, butterfly sleeves,
Breck girl hair.
And I dress up for Him.
The navy coat with gold buttons
that waits all week, sighing.
I'm seven, and still chew my hair.
I make the world
with each click
of my black buckle shoes.

Sunday school – my chair rears up on its
hind legs, a stallion I am
taming. I'm good with wild things,
patient, fearless. Repeat:

Now I lay me down to sleep,
I pray the Lord my soul to keep...
(But death is a nothing, a nonsense word;
my life a party that no one ever leaves...)

Falling is like waking up.
The strings are cut.
My teacher lifts me from the floor,
rights my chair.
I cry because
no one caught me.
Nothing held me there.

Korea

We are four sealed containers
in thin light.
Sound fills the room
like water.
Waves of babble-hiss.

5:00 The Flintstones
5:30 The Brady Bunch
6:00 News

Inside us, corrosive liquids
threaten to dissolve walls,
spill, drown.
Outside us, sunset, lime –
delicious colours that never were.

8:00 The Little House on the Prairie
*9:00 M*A*S*H*

Colonel Blake's fishhook hat
merges with the crown of thorns
shown to us in Sunday School.
Where is Korea? Is Jesus there?
Why do men shoot each other?

10:00 Kojak

Time frets at our seals.
Dad says he's seen this one before.

It's all reruns now.

Honey

I fold myself small as a postage stamp.
I crawl under the table.
I hide from the sky
I hide from eyes
I hide from everything
that will take me away.

Mother spreads honey on bread.
She is singing.
I stare at her knees,
large ruddy circles.
Mom, sing that song for me.
Don't let me leave you.
Keep me inside
your warm yellow kitchen.

I am invisible
but when she is finished
she passes the honeyed bread
to my cupped fingers
in the shadows
between the cold silver legs.

Mom, keep singing.
I am your daughter.

I am an empty room

The bed is a white grave;
the square-jawed walnut suite
are mourners, heads bent.
The bone coloured curtains closed.
The blue walls, waiting.

Silent.
The dog-eared copy of *The Joy of Sex*
muffled beneath crisp pillowcases
in the bottom dresser drawer.

Clean.
The sheets with vague sepia stains
banished to the back of a shelf.

Bloodless.
The red Valentine once taped to the mirror
taken down, never replaced.
A yellowing slice of tape
reminds.

Fourteen

John Lennon is dead
and I hate everyone.
Mom undercooks the pancakes so
a grey glue leaks from them,
merging with the syrup.
My brother says he likes them runny,
and eats them.
Suck-up!
Mom purrs.

Three is always
two-and-one.

Dad lives one bus
and two subway stops away,
so I am Harvey-in-the-morning's girl.
Q102 FM.

I'm a smoker I'm a toker
Instant Karma's gonna getcha
Gonna shoot
the whole day down.

A dial twist from mom's station,
"WMGK,
where the magic is the music!"
Q102 is permanent dusk;
purple shaded,
sidewalk breathing,
tickle bellied twilight,
when pale painted vampires like me
lope down South Street
rehearsing for apocalypse

in doorways.
Kissing the world goodbye
every night.

How annoying
to find it still there in the morning.

dis

(After Caitríona O'Reilly)

I will swallow anything.
Like a snake devouring
an ostrich egg,
distended, eyes cold;
disengaging from its
swollen, stretched,
distorted belly,
its masticating
jaws,
the sour
dismal stench of its breath
that rises like hot smog
above a
dismantled city.

Chill and dark in my small room,
coiled here on the floor. Around me,
spoon scraped cartons and
discarded wrappers form
a lip of debris,
a tidemark;
this is how high the water was,
this time.

Shirt

A silken splurge.
Color of loyalty.
Shade of serenity.
Summer sky blue.
It glides
over the pouting
flesh of his arms.
Floats
into place across
the gassy globe of his belly.
He's ready.
Sucks in his gut as he
steps out the door onto
Chestnut Street.
The yellow dust
of civilization.
Traffic's savage music, the cruel
flash of sun stroked metal,
a thousand shuffling feet.
His shirt protects him
from the siege of stares.
From the panting subway grate,
the bony billboard model,
the exhaust.
He feels almost safe;
bravely, belly first, he meets
the heat-soaked day.

Hampshire College Halloween

Wearing prom pink with white gloves, I was hypnotised by
                             my skirt spinning.
Chuck and Mike were lazing on this bench –
                             the moon was silver.
And Andy walked by, dressed as Jesus in a long white toga, hair wavy
                             like a midnight ocean.
And he was carrying this crazy cross, big as him, and it was
                             white in the moonlight.
And Andy said "hey" and we said "hey", and then Chuck got up
and he was walking behind Andy,
                             matching step for step.
And I said, "Watcha doin'?" and Chuck said,
                             "Following Jesus, Dude."
And we giggled and got in line and then we were all followers of Jesus.
                             And Jesus led.
And if Jesus drank, we drank; and if Jesus danced, we danced;
                             and if Jesus did a bong hit,
                             we praised Jesus,
and did one right after Him. And we fell around giggling
                             and Jesus giggled too.
And He led us through the silvered night, and we were free;

                             and no one got nailed to anything.

The Goddess and the Chickpea

for my brother

I came home from college all
cappuccino this, cappuccino that.
Queried why ShopRight
didn't carry goat's cheese.
Scandalized Dad
by going braless at the
International House Of Pancakes.
I had big ideas.
Something about feminism
and tofu. The zeal
to tutor heathen natives
on the Goddess and the chickpea.

At my same age, Dad was in Toledo
sleeping in his car.
Mom a clerk
who lunched at Woolworth's counter
on tomato soup made
from ketchup and hot water.
You and I, as straight-faced kids
ate Spam on tombstones
of Wonder Bread
with government issue cheese.

Then I looked up.
Got my first
glimpse of sky...

I have since forgotten the Goddess
though remain partial
to the chickpea.

You still don't trust cappuccinos –
think they are mostly
froth.

Winter, Eggs

I thought of Denice
in the deli section of Atkin's Market
because she used to work there
(I saw her, for an instant,
under the fluorescence, in that stupid red
apron Mr. Atkins made her wear.)
And I thought, don't forget to call her,
and did I remember the eggs?

Walking uphill, into the wind,
hugging the groceries, scarred
and shrivelled apples from the orchard
underfoot. I'm trying to name the song
that was on the Muzak.
Thinking also of an omelette
and a strong cup of coffee.
A winter lunch.

Gretchen is waiting at the top of the driveway –
too pale, not waving, hugging her body,
where is her coat?
When I reach her, she tells me,
"Put down the groceries,"
so I balance them on the hood of a car.
" – something to tell you. Denice – "
Call her. Eggs. Got them.
" – was on that plane. That we saw
on the news."

Grass on fire.
Seatbelts hanging from trees.
The groceries start to slide.
Gretchen steadies them.
My voice is like ice creaking
and shattering under our feet.

I remember.
The song on the Muzak was "Fire and Rain",
and I saw her, for an instant,
her brown arms on the counter,
giggling with me about Hank Armstrong.
Asking if I wanted to go swimming
at the reservoir, when she got off work.
But that was summer.
We are deep in winter now.
The reservoir is silent, choked with ice.
I remembered the eggs, and I came home
and next I would have called her.

We head inside. Gretchen carries
the groceries.
Later, she puts them away.
Snowy white eggs, whole and perfect.
Safely away in the refrigerator.

Bay Area Rapid Transit

tracks tracks tracks empty
nowhere going
of sick is she
receiver dangling
from up up up drifts
tiny tinny voice
his
moving thing only
the station of length
paces receiver
and cigarette drops drops drops
listen just
listen just
ever
he can't
why
belly her in wound hot
from up words her
drags woman
the tracks empty
patience patience
our for us thanks thanks
speakers unseen from down drifts
voice voice payphone into swears
heat the in words hard hard
wrings and smokes and leans lipstick
smeared with woman patience
patience our
for us thanks
thanks thanks thanks thanks
thanks speakers unseen
from down down drifts
voice

listen just
listen just
ever he can't
why
tracks empty
empty

Rain Again

First awake, she moves
to the window on shuddering
foal's legs
and parts the curtains silently in time
to the metronome of his breath.

The rhythm reminds her
of wiper blades, squeaking
their song.

Family car trips.
Her parents sat,
locked in silent combat, seething
in the pilot and co-pilot seats.

Herself puddled in the back
in cold, blinking
submarine light.

She parts the curtains
while the man who loved her yesterday
sleeps on, in what remains
of their pooled body heat.

She parts the curtains.
Rain again.

Falling Alone

He can't find his face
in the bathroom mirror.
The glass is foggy.

He thinks about that tree –
the one in the forest
that falls silently
because it falls alone.

He traces her initials
in the steam.

Morning Kisses

Your glasses are on the shelf by the clock,
carelessly forgotten.
I keep seeing your face
floating behind them.
You leave pieces of yourself everywhere.

Today the coffee will be potent.
Not your tired, spent brew,
but alive, like blood and smoke,
the way I like it.
I take down a single mug,
turn my back on last night's dishes,
and open the back door.

A halo of birdsong
encircles my head.
The sky is gold, ripe with promise.
The jasmine plant my landlady tends
stains the air with sweet, wild, fragile scent.
My hands, stained with coffee grounds,
look like a gardener's hands.
The early air is soft and damp on my face,
and I thank the sky

for morning kisses.

Open Palms

i.

I dream of my dead
daughter.
I find her
buried under the cradling
roots of the maple tree –
silver skinned, flat boned
coiled and shuddering
in troubled sleep.
Salvageable.
With my hands
I excavate her.

Tilt the face
(a cold sliver of moon)
and breathe pink breath
into silver.
I wait
for her
unfolding,
her startled birth cry.

The man beside me
does not help me.
Instead,
like a bather testing the warmth of his bath,
he dips his toe into the dirt.
Then, with his soft palms,
pats a blanket of soil
in place over his shoes.
"How would it feel to be dead?" he muses.
"How would it feel…", as stars lurch
and rain down like daggers,
"How would it feel to be…?"

ii.

He holds his newspaper like a shield,
half lowered.
I sit beside him,
avoid the flickering heat
of his eyes,
lose myself again
in the mane of his hair, copper-gold,
maple leaves in the last warm light
of an Autumn afternoon.
I am not well.
I breathe too fast,
my hands can't seem to close
around anything.
Pencils, spoons
and house keys drop away
from my aching open fingers.
Facts and hard won insights slip away,
beyond my grasp.

I want him
to wake me from my troubled sleep.
To press his soft, open palms
to my face, as he did once,
when checking me for fever.
I want him to
find me.

But his smile eats all the oxygen in the room,
and I am strangled blue
by the time he tells me
that everyone loves me.

iii.
I dream he is murdered.
The yard scarred
with the boot prints of soldiers
deep and sharp.
In the tall grass I find the head
of our German Shepherd, still
faithfully watching.

A purple wailing echoes
inside the house.
And he is there,
alone and moaning,
poisoned, gassed,
blue and dying.
He does not know why.
His soft palms fall open to the rain of stars.

The shrieking choir is silenced.
He is still
faithfully watching…

A child rises
from his body.
She is my daughter,
a silver vapour,
the last
shadow he casts.
And she is smiling.
"I miss him," I tell her,
and in her father's soft, rusted voice,
she says,
"I'm right here."

Home from Work

The red rug floats like a postcard
on the cold lake of linoleum.
There's a mocking beard of dust
on the typewriter cover.
Unread post, unread papers,
heartbeat blink of answering machine;
worlds and voices and questions, caged
on a toy sized tape.
Kitchenette:
a garlic bulb baker,
and a martini shaker, and the
single, veiny blue bowl bought at Pier One.
Oily cartons on the counter still smell
of plum sauce.
In the fridge, food hardens, curls
at the edges,
and gin, and olives, and always ice.
Neighbours' argument echoes
down the heating duct. A door slams,
a name is called, twice.
Chrome table legs capture last light.
Bedroom:
television clicked on,
like a fire in a cave.
Over the bed, tin Christmas angels.
All year round.
Canned laughter. That perfect sized hollow
in the mattress. That perfect first sip.
Darkness comes. Digital clock,
red numbers watching.

Floating on the cold lake.

Silk Scarf

Bought in a store
full of beautiful, useless things
on 24th Street. New Year's Eve.
Something to make up for my
cheap heels and suntan pantyhose,
my office-girl-packed-lunch life.

To rustle, thin as skin, purple
and the deep resolved green
of currency. Like stained glass
when light moves through it.
Cost more
than my dress.

Wore it to a swanky do
in a suite at the Fairmount;
friends of friends, vaguely showbiz,
sipping from elaborate glasses
while I tottered
on my cheap heels

and prayed to be noticed.
Prayed not to be noticed.
To be, just this once,
beautiful and useless...

Number Five

Many people at Number Five
will say there's too many
at Number Five –
cardiganned aunties in cruel beehives
will say there's no room
in Number Five.
Grey faced uncles, barely alive
will say there's no air
inside Number Five.
Sharp elbowed floozies, too drunk to drive
teeter and totter
around Number Five.
Six empty suits have only arrived
to smoke and pace
inside Number Five.

And one soft man with pallbearer eyes
misplaced his sweetheart
inside Number Five.
He searches each room for her feathery smile,
her cool soft arms that wait all the while
but he's lost her, amongst the sad
and the vile
that crowd into Number Five.

And many people at Number Five
will say there's too many
At Number Five –
shop worn Sallies crowd the drive,
babies on hips,
outside Number Five.

And young men turn old
and are sad to survive
the death of their purpose,
the dusk of their pride –
and they stumble on sadly, sadly alive
in the din of
Number Five.

Better Days

Inside the trailer, it's hot.
Her husband inspects her Inbox,
clicks Delete, Delete
Delete. She makes coffee,
reassures,
adds sugar.

Once she and I touched hands,
danced badly, smoked weed,
burned bacon, ate soft eggs
off mismatched plates.
Wrote our names in window steam.
Dreamed of perfect guys, cups with saucers,
better days.

Sky Multiplied By Two

Hands.

I told you I was leaving my body for a while,
and would you keep an eye on it while I was gone?

Black women dance in bright Sunday hats.
Wind chimes, jasmine. Safe.

A tide of lifted hands.

The palm trees made you sad; like us,
they'd been transplanted.
I miss knowing about your life.

Soy mochas. Everyone in black,
no one in a hurry. Tim's red jeep. The bay.
Cabernet jewel bright. Sinking through the afternoon.
This city is ours.

Tide. Sudden turn.

Virginia Woolf's diaries, water pistol fish.
Crusty bread dripping with anchovies.
A tiny violin for the Christmas tree.

Sudden turn, sky

multiplied by two. The beating,
the white spray.
The ocean is here.
Here, too.

I miss knowing about your life.

Part Two

To Sylvia Plath

I mistook your
open graves
for cathedrals.

Paid my pennies
and lit candles inside.
I thought you were
very brave.

At twenty-nine I tried to die.
Shredded by my need
for work that mattered, clothes that fit,
a face glad to see me.

This need had no dignity –
lay naked,
legs spread,
howled and stank.

Maybe I did die,
to be wombed in the cabin of a jet,
its landing screech and jolt
my birth cry.

Learning to walk the second time
is harder.
I can't forget how it hurts
to fall.

I've come back to myself,
someone else.
I think I am
very brave.

Salthill

Thin bands of cloud
measure the moon –
hands on a great gold clock.

Like the tide
       we retreated
and returned.

Your fingers curl
around mine, and press;
sand and water
in darkness, embrace.

Trafalgar Square

Yes, she tells him, yes.
I gush, pour, kiss.
My white foam touches
the sky.
My hissing jets do their liquid dance,
casting spray on these lovers in the city.

Two lovers in the city.
His eyes drink her *yes* –
in his thirst he has to kiss
her, feel faith in her touch.
He whispers thanks to the listening sky.
Two begin their dance.

Red buses dance.
The spires and domes of the city
gather and reflect her *yes*.
The sun will kiss
the countless windows gold, its touch
a wedding blessing from the sky.

School trip kids in pairs beneath the sky
giggle and fidget and dance
across this soft centre of the city,
and yes, yes, she tells him, *yes*.
The children smirk at their nervous kiss,
the sudden clumsiness of their touch.

I soar and splash in daylight's touch.
I bounce off the blue rim of sky.
The April breeze asks me to dance –
just a plain Friday in the city.
But yes, she told him. And that *yes*
is a birth; a spell; a parade; a kiss.

And all of London puckers for that kiss!
Taxi men get giddy under love's touch.
Tourists cartwheel across the sky.
Waitresses drop their trays and dance,
businessmen jitterbug around the city,
stirred by eternal *yes*.

A clutzy kiss, a quiet yes
have rearranged the sky I touch –
over the plain city, above the endless dance.

The Wellspring Wife

(after Pushkin)

It is a tradition in St. Petersburg for newlyweds to be photographed by
the Bronze Horseman, a statue of Peter the Great astride his horse.
The statue overlooks the River Neva.

Neva whispers in her sleep
as Peter's city rises
in Summer's arms.
I drip lace.
My veil lifts in the breeze
like the foam of a wave.
I am the Wellspring Wife –
I blow kisses
and bring floods.

I am the Wellspring Wife,
barefoot on Decembrists' Square.
My groom beside me
tugs on his tie.
We smile into the lens.
I shape stones
quench thirst
swallow sailors whole.
Don't tell him.

I am the Wellspring Wife
and all Peter fears.
His horse rears at the scent
of briny me.
Under men's constructions
the restless water rises.
I am the Wellspring Wife.
I seep into cracks
lick at the foundations
bide my time.

My Husband, the Great Poet

My husband, the great poet.
Beneath his shirt lies the skin of a poet,
mushroom pale; it last saw the sun
the day Nixon left the White House.
Above his shirt lies the jumper of a poet,
with a pattern
that can be seen
from outer space.

My husband, the sensitive poet.
His favourite book is *The Collected Verse
Of Alcoholic Russian Writers
Who All Eventually Topped Themselves*.
He reads to me from it
on bank holidays.

My husband, the political poet.
He slides into bed beside me
(woolly socks still on)
and stokes my fire with breathy whispers
about the collapse
of modern
socialism.

My husband, the networking poet.
He does not believe in God;
nevertheless,
he keeps The Divine E-mail Address on file, just in case.
And when Jesus returns to his flock on Earth,
He will phone my husband first,
to ask for a reading at Sheridan's
and a write-up in the Advertiser.

My husband, the glamorous poet.
He has read to spellbound crowds
in Ballina and Chelmsford.
I, meanwhile, wash his tea stained mug,
peg his washing to the line –
watch the arse actually fall
out of his trousers.

My husband, the worldly poet.
When he returns, he makes for me
a four-star romantic meal.
Sometimes he even changes
the oil in the chip pan.

My husband, the great poet.
After dinner, he puts on Andy Williams
singing *The Impossible Dream*
and winks at the cat, and takes me in his arms,
and dances me across the lino…

My poet. The great husband.

Part of Me

...is here amidst the glasses
and shiny hardback covers, part of me toys
with my fork and orders the watercress soup,
smiles
into the blue evening,
white sails caterpillared across the Marina.
Part of me blinks at the TV actor,
the singer-songwriter, the Nobel Laureate.
Every conversation is a Gerber daisy,
opening to the sun.
Here in my lace shawl,
legs swinging
beneath the heavy tablecloth;
the child allowed at the grownups' table.
Part of me is here by the grace of God
and good people, friends in common,
amidst the thick perfume
of coffee and cleverness.
Success is a white
stranger on the stairs
who might, or might not,
be beckoning.

Part of me is still
at home in silence,
thin smoke drifting
from an extinguished candle.
My toes curled in damp socks,
the bed a tattered raft.
Part of me makes instant anything,
envies the microwave bulb
its definite glare,
wonders if I'm still emitting

any rays at all.
Mutes the phone
so when it doesn't ring
it is only part of my plan.
Part of me
talks to myself
about waiting for buses
that never come;
avoids sitting
in your empty chair.

And wherever you are,
how ever many people
slurp your words, and
pat your back;
how ever many hulking cars
line the curb, waiting to take you
anywhere you want to go…
part of me is always
climbing in beside you.

And part of me is always
somewhere else.

On Not Getting Nominated

Disappointment is a cold bath.
We step out shrivelled,
blue-lit, blood slow,
genitals
dysfunctional –
scrubbed of poise,
stripped of smugness,
naked as the indifferent day
we first slid into the white world
and wailed –
inconsequentially.

On My Mother's Street

The moon sniggers.
The houses spit.
The darkness slaps.
The trees point and laugh.

They mean it,
all mean it,
they will hurt you
if you let them.
She told me.

I wish I could
remember where
I live.

Newcastle Road

November's paper skin
is stretched taut.
On Newcastle Road I meet
the man who's building a house
out of twilight.
His breath is soured
by the fumes of ancient rage.
He stalks past, cellophaned
flowers across his chest;
disappears inside the hospital.

I mutter a prayer
to no one,
rush home
to light the lamps –
pull curtains
against the empty sky.

Cathal, Briefly

The last time
I saw you
I said we were like
two old soldiers.
You smiled
with your whole face.

If I had known
your war was over;
that you had said,
Enough.

If I had seen
in your white smile
the ragged flag
of surrender…

But the last time
I saw you
I was glib,
useless.
Met Cathal, briefly
I wrote in my journal.
The last time.

To a Writer I Used to Know

For you, ambition
is a four-alarm fire;
envy the horsewhip
that forces you on.
Your gossip is slug pellets
dipped in brown sugar;
too bad your poems
aren't as sweet or as strong.

Inside you, jealousy
crushes you breathless
like the squeeze
of a bony and blue veined hand.
Beside you, your baby
wails into nothing.
Your eight-year-old son
is a worried old man.

Crocodile Sonnet

I'm being hugged by a crocodile,
trapped in his leathery grip.
Lord, but his breath is so briny and vile!
His reptile claws threaten to rip
the flesh from my back if I pull away.
I force myself to cling like a lover.
His skin is cold and greeny-grey.
I grimace and wish this all was over!
His teeth have torn tougher meat than me,
I think, as his snout presses into my neck.
I glimpse his spinning eyes as he
gives my cheek a quick social peck.
"Congrats!" he smirks, with a courtly half-bow.
"Love the book! What are you working on now?"

Poets Are Just Like Everyone Else

Today over breakfast
Husband and I discussed
the rhyme scheme of Petrarchan
sonnets –
its merits, relative to
the Shakespearean style.

I sipped my cappuccino
thoughtfully.
Husband stroked
our cat.
It was an edifying
conversation.

After which, Husband and I
scaled the drapes
and batted at invisible
birds.
Our cat sighed,
tidied his whiskers and
kept reading the Guardian.

Zelda Fitzgerald Holding Her Cat

She is leaning forward slightly,
the cat's paw draped faithfully
across her arm.

Skin pale and smooth,
in flat, fading afternoon light.
Angry bones beneath.

Eyebrows artfully shaped –
how can I make you see her eyes?
Picture black storm clouds –

no, never mind.
Just picture eyes.
Sharp, dark, wary.

Her expression welcomes,
does not trust.
Her lips have considered a smile,

decided against it.

Karma the Cat

Spring without your nose
burrowed in white star jasmine
blossoms, breathing in.

Without your muddy
paws printing dark galaxies
across the pink sheets.

We used to sprawl out,
queens in green communion,
two sun worshippers.

Your triangle ears
listened to liquid silver
sound of our windchimes.

Your so certain eyes
wise as the grass.
I watched them close.

Big Pink Umbrella

I am:
Tax bills and spin cycles
Non-drowsy cough syrup
All out of bin bags
Photocopied lesson plans
Running late

You are:
In your pajamas
Sighing on the third stair.
"Nothing tastes of anything",
You will tell me
When you ring.

But you don't ring.

And I think that you think
I'm busy just to mock you.
That my life opens up,
Like a big pink umbrella,
And I'm dancing ahead of you,
And you're getting wet.

What Seems To Be The Problem?

It's written all over my body.
My breasts and neck scorched,
no maiden's blush
but fingers of flame, such as once
devoured witches.
My scalp too tight.
My heart judders.
My sleep torn open
by panic-bird talons.
Bald patches on my memory.
After hundreds of cycles, my blood's
gone shy, withdrawn
like the nervous girl at a party,
who hides herself in the loo.

It's written all over my body,
but illegible
to the woman who studies my chart
looking for loopholes –
distracted by coughs
in the waiting room.

I've done my homework;
kept track of dates,
interviewed aunties,
graphed hormonal history.
I know this is the start
of the marshy autumn
between tart and crone.

It's written all over my body,
but she is illiterate.

Ten years my junior,
a cheerleader type.
She closes my file.
I shrink
to the size of a single
ticked box.

She leans forward
in the confiding pose
they taught her in school
and recommends
stress management.
She smiles, and says
try yoga!

As she glad-hands me
out the door
I think about bashing
her blonde head in
with her
framed diploma.
How's that
for stress management,
honey-bunch?

Daughter

*There is no more sombre enemy of good art
than the pram in the hall.* – Cyril Connolly

You are such a quiet child,
muddy, soft,
still part animal;
kneeling in the back yard
wielding a plastic spade,
chewing your bottom lip.
Un-earthing worms.
Stripes of dirt under your nails.
Your head just a little
too big for your body.
Your jacket Christmas red.

Letters make words, lines, music –
you.
I close the book.
You are unmade.
The chance we couldn't take.
The plastic spade vanishes.
The child who would only wail
if I tried to work on a poem.
The hole in the back yard fills.
Your muddy tracks on the kitchen floor peel away.

I'm not sure I'm big enough
to hold the words and you –
you would suffer
for my smallness.

Your red jacket fades into cold cloud.
The fragrance of your hair becomes
the scent of promised rain.
The worms burrow, undisturbed.

Daisy

I take up space
with my sun-freckled brow,
my fat French lips, my fat
American vowels –
"to-MAY-to,
a-LOO-min-um,
MAWL" –
my love bitten neck,
my big fat thighs, my
PERSONALITY
soft as the sheen of sweat.
I take up space, sip coffee.
The café is dead
at this hour, late sun captive
in glass.

They take up space
with their proper posture, shrill
lipstick, brittle
opinions propped up by
distinguished gentlemen,
distant or dead;
themselves propped up by
extinguished gentlemen,
fucked up or fled.

They take up space,
these women and their ghosts.
They summon the waitress,
sip tea,
glare at me.

They think I take up
too much space.
That I ruined
my husband, *the poor lad* –

and I have, it's true,
ruined him, like
a suburban lawn is ruined
by the daisy's
wide awake eye.

Supermarket Selves

I cried by the canned goods
at twenty two;
trying to decide if
I was a vegetarian.
Too many choices then.
I don't know how
I got here.
Embarrassed by the lushness
of oranges.
Fingers clenched on coins,
counting, counting.
Coveting Korma sauce,
€2.69 a jar.

Funny to think
how vast is the supermarket.
A universe of fresh fish,
frozen waffles. But I can't see
all that under
this sky of sallow stars, clutching
the wire basket childless
women carry.
I can't see the universe
when I'm inside it.
All I can see
is this aisle I'm on.